BONE HEAD

Story of the Longhorn

Desiree Morrison Webber

Line Illustrations by
Sandy Shropshire

EAKIN PRESS ⚡ Austin, Texas

To Steve

COVER: "Maverick" by Chad Payne. Cross Timbers Studios, Route 2, Box 74, Duncan, OK 73533. 580-255-6111.

FIRST EDITION
Copyright © 2003
By Desiree Morrison Webber
Published in the United States of America
By Eakin Press
A Division of Sunbelt Media, Inc.
P.O. Drawer 90159 🖃 Austin, Texas 78709-0159
email: sales@eakinpress.com
🖳 website: www.eakinpress.com 🖳
ALL RIGHTS RESERVED.
1 2 3 4 5 6 7 8 9
1-57168-763-7 (HB)
1-57168-750-5 (PB)

Library of Congress Cataloging-in-Publication Data
Webber, Desiree, 1956–
  Bone head: story of the longhorn / by Desiree Morrison Webber ; line illustrations by Sandy Shropshire.– 1st ed.
    v. cm.
  Includes bibliographical references (p.).
  Contents: Bad-tempered gold—Fighting wolves—Outlaws on the trail—Texas Fever!—On the Chisholm Trail—Roping and branding wild bone heads—Stampedes and fearsome rivers—Good-bye, longhorned critters—Model Ts and crated longhorns.
    ISBN 1-57168-763-7
    1. Longhorn cattle—Southwestern States—History—Juvenile literature. 2. Texas longhorn cattle—Southwestern States—History—Juvenile literature. [1. Longhorn cattle. 2. Texas longhorn cattle.]
I. Shropshire, Sandy, ill. II. Title.
SF199.L6W43   2003
636.2'8–dc21   2002156398

CONTENTS

Acknowledgments

My thanks to the following individuals and institutions: Claudine Daniel and Joe Kimball of the Wichita Mountains Wildlife Refuge, Deborah Baroff of the Museum of the Great Plains, Melecia Caruthers and Kitty Pittman of the Oklahoma Department of Libraries, the Denver Public Library, the Fort Worth Public Library, the Oklahoma Historical Society, Chisholm Trail Heritage Center in Duncan, Oklahoma, Gin Dodson of the Chisholm Trail Historical Museum, Eva Poole of the Denton Public Library in Denton, Texas, Fran Cook of the Grace Pickens Public Library in Holdenville, Oklahoma, Bonnie Crawford of the Okemah Public Library in Okemah, Oklahoma, Western History Collections at the University of Oklahoma, Luann Waters—Chisholm Trail tour guide extraordinaire, A. J. Smith of *The Oklahoma Cowman*, Chad Payne, and Molly Levite Griffis.

Chapter 1

BAD-TEMPERED GOLD

"I'll never forget my first try at night-herding," wrote Jesse James Benton. "All of sudden, for no reason I could see, the herd were up and in full gallop in a stampede and us cowboys after them . . . You could hear those big horns popping and rattling and the roar of their hoofs in a sound you can't describe."

Jesse James Benton grew to love the cowboy life. His story is a typical cowboy tale. Like many drovers, he started herding ornery longhorns at a young age. Cattle trails were a great place for young men to earn money, to live an exciting life, and to fill their stomachs with beans and sourdough biscuits.

When Jesse was twelve years old, his mother died of a fever. He missed her dearly. With his mother gone, Jesse's pa had both farming and cooking to do. So every day the young man helped with chores around the house.

A cattle trail ran near the family's Texas homestead. Sometimes Jesse and his brother Henry would ride over to the trail in a wagon. They hoped to find

1

abandoned calves to bring home and raise. If a calf could not keep up with its mother, the cattle drovers were forced to leave it behind.

Jesse dreamed of becoming a cowpuncher. Someday he would herd bone heads northward from Texas, through Indian Territory, and into Kansas.

A year after Jesse's mom died, his dad decided to bring home a new wife. No one could replace his ma. So Jesse slipped his legs through two pairs of pants and buttoned on two shirts. It was the only way to take extra clothing. He saddled the Kentucky mare his father had given him, and behind the McClellan saddle, Jesse tied on two quilts. These blankets would be his only protection against cold weather, freezing rain, hail, sleet, wind, and dust.

A trail boss named Tobe Odem hired Jesse. For thirty dollars a month, extra horses to ride, and all the beans he could chow down, Jesse James Benton became a cowboy. But what did that mean, to become a cowboy? It meant that he had to work with the one of the meanest, ugliest, most stubborn animals on cloven hooves.

Longhorn cattle were called "bad-tempered gold" because they made people rich overnight. A steer

Longhorns had a reputation for being more dangerous to people than a grizzly bear.

2

worth $5 in Texas might bring $60 in California. Multiply a herd of 2,500 longhorns by $60 per head and you have $150,000. That kind of money bought land, big homes, silk clothes, and trips to Paris, France.

Longhorns' dangerous temper and horns caused some cowhands to meet an early grave. "The average Texas Longhorn bull was about as mean a creature as ever went on four legs," wrote Charles Martin in the late 1800s, "and the longer he lived, the meaner he became."

Before cowboys drove longhorns up cattle trails, this breed was a different type of animal. They were descendants of Spanish cattle brought to the North American continent some five hundred years earlier. Bone heads hid in the brush during the day and came out only at night to eat grass or drink water. Longhorns were not tame animals. They did not live near the barn like grandma's milk cow "Ol' Bess."

Settlers who came to Texas called the longhorns "wild cattle." Unlike domesticated cattle, wild long- horns did not travel in large herds. Cows with calves stayed together to protect one another, but bulls moved alone.

Men hunted bone heads just like they pursued deer, elk, and buffalo. Lieutenant Colonel Richard Dodge called the wild cattle "cousins of the buffalo."

Dodge wrote that tracking female longhorns was a challenge. Cows kept their mouths shut and hid in the thickets. Males, on the other hand, announced their location. "It seems impossible for the bull to keep his mouth shut," wrote Dodge, "and when not actually eating he is bellowing or moaning or making some

hideous noise which indicates his whereabouts to the hunter."

Just because it was easy to find a bull did not mean it was easy to kill one. Bulls were mean, fearless, and ready to fight—a dangerous combination. They were known to chase hunters up trees or to attack entire groups of people.

General Zachary Taylor's army was marching from Corpus Christi, Texas, to Matamoros, Mexico, in 1846. One soldier spotted a wild bull standing just a short distance away. He fired at the animal but only wounded it. Angry as lion with its tail on fire, the longhorn charged.

The soldier fled for the safety of his comrades. He hoped that the large number of men would scare the animal away. Instead, the bull plunged into the column of soldiers and scattered them like ants. After snorting and thrashing about, the beast finally left Taylor's army alone.

Who would guess that just ten years later, men would start to drive these wild longhorns along cattle trails? Cowhands herded these crazy creatures all the way from Texas to California, New York, Kentucky,

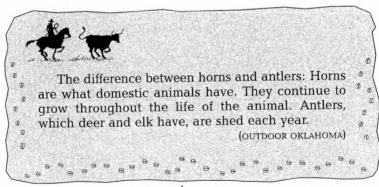

The difference between horns and antlers: Horns are what domestic animals have. They continue to grow throughout the life of the animal. Antlers, which deer and elk have, are shed each year.

(OUTDOOR OKLAHOMA)

and Illinois. If people were willing to pay money for longhorn cattle, the cowboys found a way to get the animals to them.

After a while, these 1,200-pound ill-tempered bone heads became famous. They carved out the Wild West! If not for longhorns, there might never have been American cowboys, chuck wagons, or trail drives.

Cowboys sang songs about the longhorns. Historians told their story. Painters glorified their spirit. Few animals have ever attracted such attention. Ready-made weapons protruded from their heads. Sharp and sturdy, their horns could pierce the leg of a rider and continue through into his horse. Their tough "bad boy" reputation was earned right from the beginning and has stayed with them to this very day.

Chapter 2

Fighting Wolves

During the 1850s, Noah Smithwick raised live-stock. He observed that his tame milk cows bolted for home when attacked by wolves but that wild long-horns fought back.

"Some of these cattle were very handsome brutes," wrote Smithwick, "coal black and clean limbed, their white horns glistening as if polished."

One evening, just as the sun glowed red in the west, Noah's wife looked out across the prairie. Their

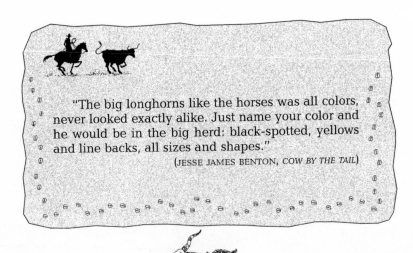

"The big longhorns like the horses was all colors, never looked exactly alike. Just name your color and he would be in the big herd: black-spotted, yellows and line backs, all sizes and shapes."

(JESSE JAMES BENTON, *COW BY THE TAIL*)

milk cows were running toward the house. Two large wolves snapped at their heels. Fleet as an antelope, a single gray wolf could pull a large cow to the ground with its powerful jaws. Wolves were fearsome predators.

"One cow, falling a little behind the band, was seized by the foremost of the wolves," wrote Smithwick, "but her calls for help caused the other cattle to turn and fight the fierce brutes back. The cows then started again for home, but the wounded one again fell behind and again was seized, but she managed to tear herself loose."

Unlike milk cows, longhorn cows refused to run. Instead they faced their foe. Females formed a ring around their calves and presented a line of horns to any wolf that dared approach.

"A wild cow takes the most anxious care of her calf," wrote Lieutenant Colonel Richard Dodge, "and is transformed by maternal instinct from one of the most timid of animals to a most daring and desperate combatant."

Longhorn females attacked cougar, wolf, or man if they ventured too close to their calves. They also displayed a strong sense of smell in tracking their young. And, if a cow lost track of her calf in a stampede, she stopped and bawled until it was found.

Charles Goodnight, a famous Texas rancher, told of

one female longhorn that walked twenty miles to find her calf. The cow had given birth while Goodnight's outfit was branding cattle in the Panhandle of Texas. Goodnight told his cowhands to move downriver the next day. He also ordered the camp cook to carry the cow's newborn bull in his wagon. The cook forgot and left the little fellow behind.

The herd had traveled ten or twelve miles before it was discovered that the calf was missing. Foreman John Farrington decided to ride back and rescue it. Without its mother, the young animal would starve to death or fall prey to wolves.

Farrington found the bull. He was waiting patiently for his mother to return. The foreman picked him up and straddled him across his saddle.

Upon returning to the herd, Farrington could not locate the mother. She had escaped to find her offspring.

Farrington left the young animal at camp and turned back to look for the mother. Ten miles out, he spotted her. The mama longhorn was trotting back toward camp! Curious, Farrington hid and watched. The cow was follow-

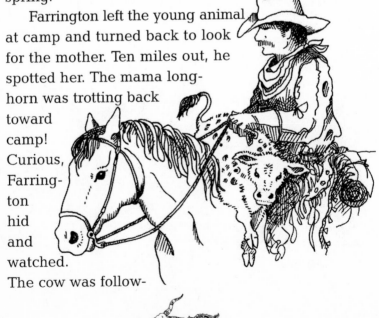

Two mother longhorns are babysitting while the other mothers take a break.

—The Oklahoma Cowman

ing his tracks. She had been trailing Farrington's horse from the scent of her calf. Back at camp, she found her little bull. Mother and child were finally reunited.

Even today, cattlemen discuss the unique care mother longhorns show their calves. Cows about to give birth will head for the thickets together. Under the cover of trees and brush, they deliver young that weigh an average of thirty-five pounds. Cows usually give birth to a single calf. Twins are rare.

When the cows need to eat grass or drink water,

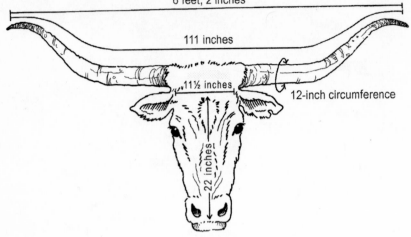

6 feet, 2 inches

111 inches

11½ inches

12-inch circumference

22 inches

one longhorn female remains in charge. She baby-sits the nursery while the other mothers take a break.

A young longhorn grows into a creature that only its mother could love. The animal's topknot is made of bone and keratin. A bone core runs three-fourths the length of each horn. Covering the core is a sheath made of keratin, similar to a human's fingernails and toenails.

These pointed projections are attached to a narrow, unattractive face, which is attached to a lanky, sway-backed body, which rests upon four skinny legs. At the end is a long, dangling tail.

View a longhorn lengthwise and it looks like a Hershey chocolate bar with two toothpicks stuck at each end.

Bulls grow horns that average three feet from tip to tip. The horns of a female are just a few inches longer. Steers, which are castrated males, produce the mightiest horns. Most steers have horn spreads as long as a

bicycle. Some have measured eight and a half feet—
longer than a living room sofa.

Although skinny as a pole, these beasts could walk
for miles and endure hardships unlike any other breed
of cattle. They were perfect animals for herding to dis-
tant destinations.

*"Champion," a very gentle longhorn steer. He traveled to Paris
in 1900 to show off his nine-foot, seven-inch spread of horns.*
—Oklahoma Historical Society

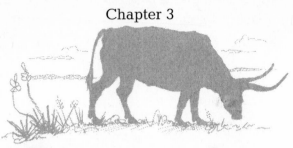

Chapter 3

Outlaws on the Trail

James Daugherty was sixteen years old in 1866. That same year, he convinced his boss to hire him and five cowboys to drive five hundred longhorn steers up the Shawnee Trail to Sedalia, Missouri.

Adventurous cattle drovers had used the Shawnee Trail since the 1850s. Heading northeast from Dallas, Texas, longhorns crossed the Red River into the Chickasaw Nation. This was Indian Territory, later known as Oklahoma. From there, cattle rambled through the rolling hills of the Choctaw, Creek, and Cherokee nations and crossed the border into Kansas or Missouri.

As James Daugherty made his way across the Indian nations, other drovers warned him to watch for trouble ahead. "Jayhawkers" were attacking cowboys and stealing their herds.

The Civil War, in which northern and southern states fought one another, had caused great sadness in many people's lives. After the war ended in 1865, some of the soldiers did not go home or did not have

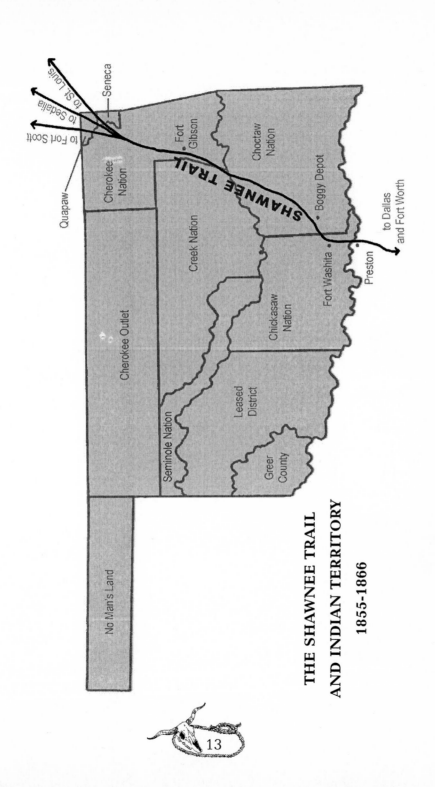

THE SHAWNEE TRAIL
AND INDIAN TERRITORY
1855-1866

13

a home to which to return. Instead they became outlaws.

Jayhawkers had been guerilla fighters for the North during the Civil War. Most Texas cowboys had fought for the South. As Texas drovers entered northern states, like Kansas, they met people who had once been their enemies.

In 1866 the Civil War had only been over for one year and feelings of hatred still ran strong. It was bad enough to meet an outlaw who wanted to steal your cattle. It was worse to meet an outlaw who was still angry about the war.

When Daugherty and his men reached the Kansas border, he instructed the cowhands to wait. He rode ahead alone to Fort Scott, Kansas. If Daugherty could sell the herd at Fort Scott, his men would not have to make the dangerous trip across Missouri to Sedalia. With luck, they could slip by the Jayhawkers unnoticed.

At Fort Scott, Daugherty found a buyer for his five hundred head of longhorns. He was to deliver them as soon as possible. But men at Fort Scott warned the young drover that it was risky business trailing cattle through this part of the country.

Daugherty returned to the herd and began the drive north. The outfit rode close to the Kansas-Missouri border. They were only a two-day ride from the fort when a mob of twenty armed men surprised them.

"One of my cowboys, John Dobbins by name, was leading the herd and I was riding close to the leader," wrote Daugherty. "Upon approach of the Jayhawkers,

14

John attempted to draw his gun and the Jayhawkers shot him dead in his saddle. This caused the cattle to stampede and at the same time they covered me with their guns and I was forced to surrender."

Unaware of the trouble ahead, the other four cowhands chased after the herd and tried to stop the stampede.

Meanwhile, the outlaws pulled Daugherty from his horse, tied him to a tree, and whipped him with hickory switches.

The gang's rough-looking appearance made them even scarier. Their leather shoes appeared to have been cut with an axe and crudely stitched together. Homemade caps of raccoon skins sat atop their heads. Their pants and shirts were constructed of rough homespun cloth.

"They began to argue among themselves what to do with me," Daugherty wrote. "Some wanted to hang me while others wanted to whip me to death."

One of the bad men stated that Daugherty was too young to be hanged. After much talking, the men finally untied the sixteen-year-old. Whipped and beaten, Daugherty pulled himself onto his saddle and rode off to find what was left of his longhorns.

The cowhands had stopped the stampede. They found some of the cattle, but one hundred and fifty head remained missing. The outlaws had stolen longhorns worth thousands of dollars.

Later that night, Daugherty and two other cowboys slipped back to bury John Dobbins. They refused to leave their friend forlorn and forgotten on the frontier. The three cut down a small tree. With the wood, they

fashioned a headboard and footboard for Dobbins' grave.

Determined not to be beaten down by outlaws, Daugherty and his men delivered the herd to Fort Scott.

Trail bosses like Daugherty sold their cattle to butchers, meat packers, military forts, and army expeditions crossing the plains. Migrants traveling to Oregon and California also bought cattle for work oxen. Cattle pulled their prairie schooners across the frontier.

Bone heads from Texas and the Indian Territory traveled as far north as New York City. Compared to the beefy breeds imported from England, the bony, sway-backed longhorns were a novelty. A reporter with the *New York Daily Times* wrote in August 1858 that the longhorns were so skinny they were barely able to cast a shadow and would not weigh anything if it were not for their horns.

Even though longhorns were funny to look at, they filled a crucial need. People living in northern states wanted beef, and Texas had plenty of it.

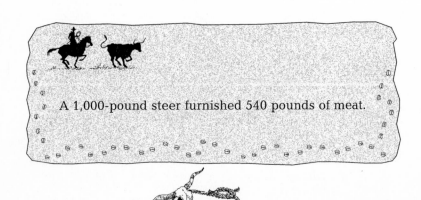

A 1,000-pound steer furnished 540 pounds of meat.

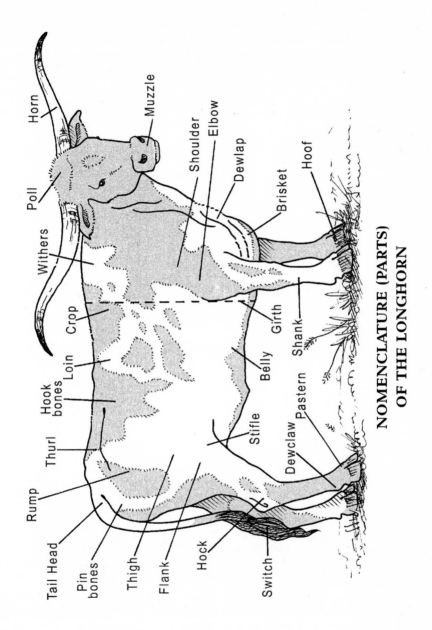

NOMENCLATURE (PARTS) OF THE LONGHORN

Horn
Muzzle
Poll
Shoulder
Withers
Elbow
Dewlap
Crop
Brisket
Loin
Hoof
Hook bones
Girth
Thurl
Belly
Rump
Shank
Tail Head
Stifle
Pin bones
Dewclaw
Thigh
Pastern
Flank
Hock
Switch

Chapter 4

TEXAS FEVER!

In 1866 a severe outbreak of Texas fever struck cattle living in Missouri and Kansas. The deadly disease caused nine out of ten infected animals to perish. Sick cattle refused to eat or drink. Their heads drooped and their eyes waxed glassy.

Hundreds of milk cows and beef cattle died, and hundreds of farmers grew angry.

What puzzled many folks was that the Texas fever did not attack longhorn cattle. Bone heads carried the illness but survived unharmed. Dr. Cooper Curtice, with the Bureau of Animal Industry, would later discover, in 1891, that a tick carried the germ that caused Texas fever. After inhabiting the southern plains for hundreds of years, the lanky critter had developed an immunity to the disease. Other breeds were not so lucky.

Ticks attached themselves to the cattle's skin using their sharp mandibles. As the ticks sucked blood from their prey, they passed along the disease.

During the 1860s, men and women did not real-

18

ize that ticks were spreading the malady. Farmers thought longhorn cattle caused the Texas fever. Wild theories blossomed in folks' imaginations.

Some people believed that bushes scratched and cut the longhorns' feet and that as the animals walked the cattle trails, blood from their hooves infected the ground. People even thought longhorns had poisonous breath, which contaminated the grass and caused other cattle breeds to become sick.

As longhorns crossed through Missouri and Kansas, they ate the grasses and lay down at night in the pastures. While they grazed and slept, the ticks crawled off of them. Then cattle belonging to nearby farmers would come to the pastures. They would eat in the same areas the longhorns had just used and pick up the ticks. Once bitten, they contracted the disease.

Texas fever took a terrible toll on the local livestock, and irate farmers demanded that something be done. Missouri and Kansas passed laws to protect their animals: Longhorns from Texas and the Indian Territory were forbidden to pass through their states.

Laws were enforced by a "shotgun quarantine." Armed farmers met the herds and ordered the cowboys to turn back.

Ranchers from Texas and the Indian nations were not about to give up on the cattle business, though. It had proved too profitable. A longhorn worth three to six dollars in Texas sold in the north for thirty to sixty dollars. One historian wrote, "During June 1866, a small lot of Texas longhorns were disposed of in Kentucky at $88 each." What a profit! At these prices,

ranchers struck it rich from their bad-tempered bone heads.

What the cattlemen needed was a new route to replace the Shawnee Trail. Farmers with weapons—and Jayhawkers with hanging ropes—made traveling through Missouri and Kansas too perilous.

In answer to the cowboys' troubles came Illinois businessman Joseph G. McCoy. During the Civil War, McCoy and his brothers had owned a livestock company. They raised and sold hogs, mules, sheep, and beef cattle.

McCoy proved a natural entrepreneur. He could smell an opportunity to make money like ants could smell a picnic.

After the war, McCoy realized that people living in the northern and eastern parts of the United Stated wanted beef. But there were not enough beef cattle, called beeves, to meet the demand. Southern cattlemen owned bone heads by

Joseph G. McCoy built stockyards in Abilene that brought cattle up the famous Chisholm Trail.

the thousands. There were nine longhorns for every man, woman, and child living in Texas.

McCoy learned of the vast number of longhorns grazing on the southern prairies. Texas drovers also told McCoy of the trouble they had met on the Shawnee Trail.

In the summer of 1867, McCoy built shipping yards, an office, a barn, and a fancy three-story hotel in Abilene, Kansas. McCoy described Abilene as "a very small, dead place, consisting of about one dozen log huts—low, small, crude affairs with dirt for roofing."

What made this "dead place" so attractive was that it sat on the Kansas Pacific Railway. Also, a flat, empty prairie surrounded the little town. And it was far, far away from farmers worried about Texas fever. McCoy imagined longhorns grazing on the acres of grass and drinking water from the nearby Solomon River.

While McCoy pictured thousands of bone heads traveling to Abilene, some railroad freighters could not understand such a dream. They may have thought McCoy had been kicked in the head by one of the mules he had raised in Illinois. One railroad company president threw McCoy out of his office: "It occurs to

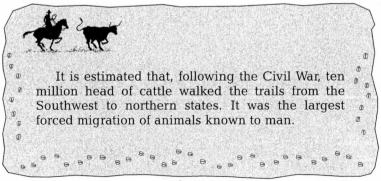

It is estimated that, following the Civil War, ten million head of cattle walked the trails from the Southwest to northern states. It was the largest forced migration of animals known to man.

21

me that you haven't any cattle to ship, and never did have any, and I, sir, have no evidence that you ever will have any, and I think you are talking about rates of freight for speculative purposes; therefore, you get out of this office, and let me not be troubled with any more of your style."

That particular gentleman was later fired. McCoy was right. The following spring of 1868, thousands of longhorns went to Abilene, Kansas.

Herds of cattle crossed the Red River into Indian Territory. Instead of heading east on the Shawnee Trail, drovers decided to try McCoy's suggested route to Abilene.

This new trail traveled through the middle of the flat, grassy plains of Indian Territory. With a whoop and a holler, cowboys drove their "little doggies" through the present-day Oklahoma towns of Waurika, Duncan, Kingfisher, Bison, Enid, and Pond Creek. Bone heads crossed the Kansas border at Caldwell and continued through the towns of Wichita, Newton, Ellsworth, and finally Abilene.

No one called the new route "McCoy's Trail" or "Joseph G.'s Trail." Drovers named the trail after someone who was no longer living.

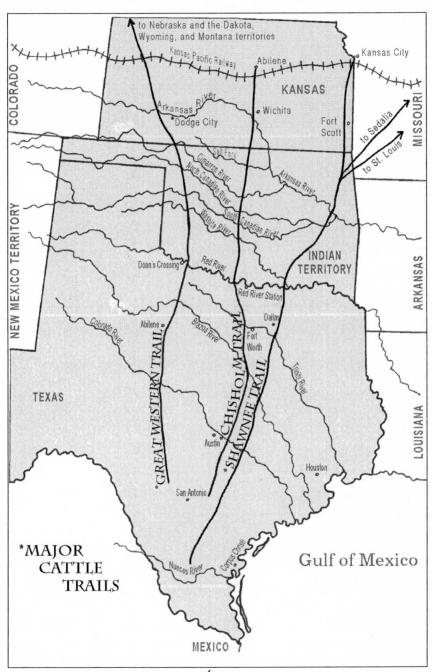

to Nebraska and the Dakota, Wyoming, and Montana territories

COLORADO

Kansas Pacific Railway

Abilene

Kansas City

KANSAS

Arkansas River

Dodge City

Wichita

Fort Scott

MISSOURI

to Sedalia

to St. Louis

Salt Fork

Cimarron River

North Canadian River

Arkansas River

NEW MEXICO TERRITORY

Washita River

South Canadian River

ARKANSAS

Doan's Crossing

Red River

INDIAN TERRITORY

Red River Station

Colorado River

Abilene

Brazos River

Dallas

Fort Worth

Trinity River

LOUISIANA

GREAT WESTERN TRAIL

CHISHOLM TRAIL

SHAWNEE TRAIL

Austin

TEXAS

Houston

San Antonio

*MAJOR CATTLE TRAILS

Nueces River

Corpus Christi

Gulf of Mexico

MEXICO

23

Chapter 5

On the Chisholm Trail

Lizzie Johnson was a cattle queen, and few women of her day could make that claim. Not only did Lizzie own longhorns, but she also registered her own brand. History records Johnson as the first woman to run her own head of cattle up the Chisholm Trail to Kansas.

Lizzie did not graduate from school to become a cattle queen. Teaching was her first passion in life. She taught math, spelling, and music for many years. To increase her income, Lizzie wrote articles for magazines and newspapers and invested her extra money in cattle. Before long, the young lady grew into a successful businesswoman. On June 1, 1871, Lizzie registered her CY cattle brand.

In 1879 Lizzie married Hezekiah Williams, a minister. After marriage she did not quit teaching, as did many women of her day. Instead, as a new bride, she opened a school on the first floor of her two-story home.

Two years after they married, Hezekiah followed his wife into the cattle business, but Lizzie kept her

income separate from her husband's. She would not share the CY brand, so he used his own ◯ road brand. Special road brands were often placed on animals before trailing them northward. These brands were burned into the hide at the shoulder or neck.

Even though their cattle companies were separate, the two used the same foreman to manage their longhorns. In an odd game of teasing, Lizzie would instruct the foreman to "steal" all of Hezekiah's calves and to put her CY brand on them. Then Hezekiah would order the foreman to steal all of Lizzie's calves and burn his brand on the little beeves.

"So the foreman was kept busy branding all of Hezekiah's calves with Lizzie's brand and all of Lizzie's calves with Hezekiah's road brand," wrote historian Emily Shelton.

Together, the devoted couple followed their herds up the Chisholm Trail—the most famous cattle trail in history.

Even though it was Joseph G. McCoy who brought thousands of longhorns up the Chisholm Trail to Abilene, Kansas, the route was named for a well-known and much-loved individual.

Jesse Chisholm was half Cherokee and half Scottish-American. He worked as a trader, freighter, and interpreter. Not satisfied with just speaking two or three languages, Jesse Chisholm spoke Cherokee, English, Spanish, Comanche, Creek, Kiowa, Kichai, Delaware, Shawnee, Chickasaw, and Choctaw. He traveled all over Indian Territory and into surrounding states.

After the Civil War, Chisholm developed a route

from Wichita, Kansas, to his Council Grove trading post in Indian Territory. Council Grove lay near the North Canadian River—not far from present-day Bethany, Oklahoma.

By running his freight wagons from Wichita to Council Grove and back again, Jesse created the original "Chisholm Trail." It was less than two hundred miles long. Once cattle drovers crossed the North Canadian River, they followed Chisholm's freight wagon ruts to Wichita. Over time, the entire trail, from Texas to Kansas, was named after Chisholm. But Jesse did not live to see it. He died in March 1868—just weeks before the first herds came up his route through Indian Territory into Kansas.

In addition to being a trader, Jesse also manufactured salt. Salt springs were located in what is now Blaine County, Oklahoma. It was here that Chisholm died. The cause of his death has remained unknown, even to this day. Jesse's friends guessed that he either ate spoiled bear's grease or ate food cooked in a brass pot.

The Chisholm Trail became so popular that it looked like a wide dirt highway from Texas to Kansas.

"We had no roads to amount to much in those days," wrote Ed Bates, who lived in north Texas. "But a cattle trail was a very conspicuous mark across the country. Sometimes it would be from fifty to one hundred yards wide, without vegetation, especially if the herds were driven along when the ground was wet."

Once longhorns crossed the Red River into Indian Territory, the trail boss rode to Monument Hills. From this knoll, he scanned the prairie. Such a vantage

26

Jesse Chisholm was born in Tennessee in 1805 or 1806. He was a quiet, gentle man respected by all who knew him. He married twice and had many children, including adopted youths whom he had rescued.

During his travels, Jesse encountered individuals who captured young slaves. Chisholm would buy the children in hopes of reuniting them with their families. If he was unable to find the parents, Chisholm adopted the young people into his own family.

Because of his ability to speak several languages, he worked as an interpreter for the military, government representatives, surveyors, and explorers. He was influential among the different Native American tribes of the Southern Plains. Many tribal members respected his opinions. Some admired him and even loved him as a brother. At Chisholm's burial, Comanche leader Ten Bears honored him. Ten Bears laid his cherished peace medal upon Chisholm's chest before he was lowered into the ground.

point showed him how many herds moved ahead and how many were behind. By the 1870s, driving cattle was big business. Several herds traveled on the trail at the same time.

Joseph G. McCoy, who started longhorns up the Chisholm Trail, advertised that the trip through Indian Territory took four weeks. Walking feisty longhorns hundreds of miles was no easy chore. Cowhands faced many challenges, including stampedes, storms, and swollen rivers. But those who rode the trails loved the rough-and-tumble life.

Chapter 6

Roping and Branding Wild Bone Heads

Nineteen-year-old Baylis Fletcher rode with a herd that began near present-day Goliad, Texas, in April 1879. Two months later the outfit had reached the Cimarron River in Indian Territory.

It had been a dry year. The Cimarron ran not as a river but as a thin, salty stream. It flowed so brackish that man and beast could barely drink it.

At the Cimarron River, the herd turned west toward Dodge City, Kansas. Ahead of them lay the Saline Reservation. Here the cattle would die if allowed to drink the salty waters, made poisonous by chemicals. The cowboys had to do everything they could to keep the bone heads from tasting the water.

"After nearly four days of trailing on the north side of the Cimarron, through a poor sandy region wooded with a straggling forest of oaks, we came to the Saline Reservation, where we were to recross the river without permitting a single animal to drink from the briny waters," wrote Fletcher.

29

Near the crossing, the cowhands gathered the herd together in a tight bunch. They had to scare the longhorns into a fast run across the water so the animals would not stop to drink. Men shook their slickers and ropes. Yelling and slapping their legs, the drovers stampeded the bone heads across the shallow riverbed.

"But once we were across, our troubles began," continued Fletcher. "The thirsty animals tried to turn back, and it was night before we got them a mile from the river. They were nearly famished. All night long they tried to escape to the river to drink. We had little rest that night. The stench from the putrid bodies of more than a hundred cattle warned us of the danger in allowing our cows to drink from the deadly waters."

The putrid animals that Fletcher described were longhorns that had arrived before his herd. These unfortunate creatures had drunk the poisonous waters and perished.

Every cattle drive was different. Each trip pre-

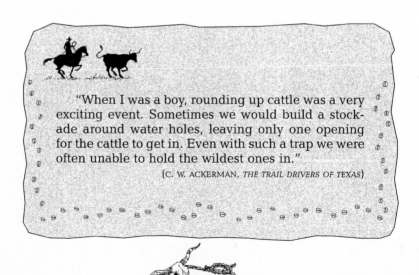

"When I was a boy, rounding up cattle was a very exciting event. Sometimes we would build a stockade around water holes, leaving only one opening for the cattle to get in. Even with such a trap we were often unable to hold the wildest ones in."

(C. W. ACKERMAN, THE TRAIL DRIVERS OF TEXAS)

sented new dangers and hardships. Cowboys strug-
gled to handle skittish longhorns during thunder-
storms, lightning, bad water, no water, outlaws, dust
storms, and stampedes.

Early cattle drives were especially difficult because drovers had to herd longhorns that were wild or
semi-wild.

Ancestors to the longhorns came from Spain in the
early 1500s. Spanish explorers and colonists brought
the animals into Mexico and later Florida and the
southwestern area of the United States. Early Spanish
settlements did not always survive. When the people
moved away, they left their cattle behind.

These creatures multiplied and changed from domestic animals to wild animals. The Spanish cattle
adapted to conditions in which the fast, wily, and
strong survived. What evolved with time and natural
selection became known as the "longhorn." Nature
demanded that it have a sleek body, with nimble feet
to run and climb quickly. Horns to fight predators
were a necessity. Wild longhorns hid in thorny
mesquite thickets during the day and came out only
at night for water and grass.

To create a herd, cowboys had to comb the brush
and timber looking for cattle. It was their job to rope
and brand longhorns that had been born in the wild or
had escaped from nearby ranches.

Cowhands captured wild longhorns by using tame
cattle. Just before dawn, cowboys would surprise
longhorns feeding in an open grassy area. Men
rushed from the timber with lassos in hand. They
roped and tied their captives. Then another crew

Cowboys branding a calf.
—Museum of the Great Plains

32

drove in a group of cattle that followed herding directions. Tame longhorns surrounded the wild ones. Once untied, most of the wild longhorns stayed with the tame herd.

When a stubborn bone head would not stay with the herd, cowboys sometimes took severe action.

"Once in a while though, we would strike an old steer that couldn't be made to stay in the herd," wrote cowboy Charles Siringo. "Just as soon as he was untied and let up he would go right through the herd and strike for the brush, fighting his way. Under those circumstances we would have to sew up their eyes with a needle and thread. That would bring them to their milk, as they couldn't see the timber."

Before heading up the trail, cowhands branded ownership markings on the animals' hides. Cowboys

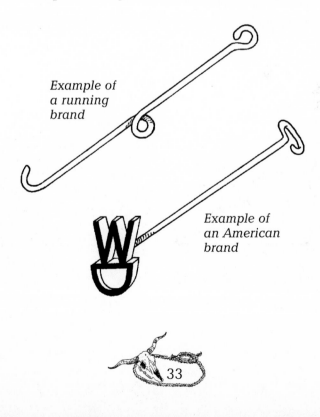

Example of a running brand

Example of an American brand

used stamp or running irons to burn designs or letters. Stamp irons pressed the design into the flesh like a hot rubber stamp. A running iron was a single rod with a bent tip. Cowboys sketched brands into hides with a running iron as if writing with a pencil.

Cattle owners had to register their brands. That way, different ranchers did not use the same brand. Sometimes people used their initials, such as DW or SS. Others created pictures—perhaps an apple or hearts. The best brand was one that could not be easily changed by cattle thieves.

Using a running iron, cattle rustlers changed brands to steal longhorns. Outlaws could change an F to an E or an O to a Q by burning another line on the animal's hide. Once the brand was changed, an outlaw claimed he owned the cattle.

In some places it was illegal to carry a running iron with you. A man caught on the trail with a running iron in his saddlebag was considered a cattle rustler. Sometimes these men were hanged on the spot.

Drovers also applied road brands to identify their herd from others found on the trail. Trail bosses often

$$F \rightarrow E$$

$$O \rightarrow Q$$

$$P \rightarrow B \rightarrow R$$

} *How running irons changed brands*

herded cattle belonging to more than one rancher. The cowboys needed a road brand to identify their herd.

Road brands were often applied to the neck or front shoulder. Riders could read the brand from horseback. Stampedes caused animals to become lost from the main herd. If a cowboy found strays in another person's herd, he proved ownership by the road brand.

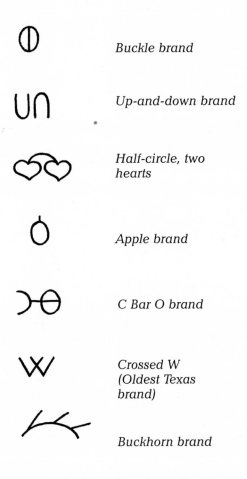

Buckle brand

Up-and-down brand

Half-circle, two hearts

Apple brand

C Bar O brand

Crossed W (Oldest Texas brand)

Buckhorn brand

Chapter 7

STAMPEDES AND FEARSOME RIVERS

On the trail, cowhands had to calm a longhorn's jumpy nature. One animal could cause the whole herd to jump up and dash away like wide-eyed, snorting fiends. When stampedes occurred, inexperienced cowboys ran into trouble.

Texas cowboy Charles Siringo recalled the story of a "short horn" from Kansas called Mr. Black. "Short horn" was Siringo's nickname for someone who worked with domestic, or shorthorn, cattle. Compared to the longhorns, with their wild and woolly dispositions, shorthorn cattle acted as tame as kittens.

Mr. Black had traveled from Kansas to purchase a herd of longhorns to drive to Kansas to sell for a profit. "After a month's hard work we had the herd of eleven hundred ready to turn over to Mr. Black who had bought them," wrote Siringo. "They were all old mossy horn fellows, from seven to twenty-seven years old.

"Mr. Black was a Kansas short horn and he had

brought his outfit of short horn men and horses, to drive the herd up the trail," wrote Siringo.

"Some of the men had never seen a Texas steer, consequently they crossed the Red River into the Indian Territory with nothing left but the grub wagon and horses. They had lost every steer and Mr. Black landed in Kansas flat broke."

A hooting owl, a barking prairie dog, or a sneezing cowboy could set off a stampede. Wild longhorns, which had just been captured from the mesquite brush, were easily spooked into a run.

Stampedes were dangerous, especially at night. Man and beast ran at blinding speed in complete darkness. Not only could a cowhand be injured or killed, but so could the longhorns he was chasing. In rough country, bone heads and horses tumbled over rocks, into creek beds, or over unseen cliffs. Prairie-dog holes led to broken legs. Horns hit trees, rocks, horses, men, and other longhorns. After a run, some

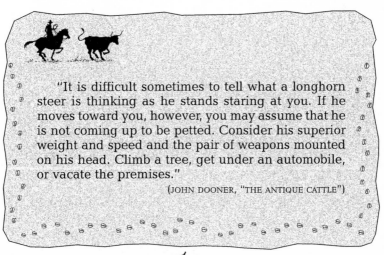

"It is difficult sometimes to tell what a longhorn steer is thinking as he stands staring at you. If he moves toward you, however, you may assume that he is not coming up to be petted. Consider his superior weight and speed and the pair of weapons mounted on his head. Climb a tree, get under an automobile, or vacate the premises."

(JOHN DOONER, "THE ANTIQUE CATTLE")

longhorns had their horns dangling by their faces like broken tree limbs.

Lightning often caused stampedes. Fluid light danced on the cattle's horns like crazed, oversized fireflies. Thunderbolts also killed many a cowhand. A cowboy on horseback was often the tallest object on the open prairie. Drovers checked their guns with the cook for safekeeping. They did not want metal increasing their chances of drawing electricity. But their precautions were not always enough.

M. A. Withers was riding in a rainstorm with two other men when tragedy struck the group. The three were traveling close together. Wither's friend, a man named Gus Johnson, rode in the center. Suddenly, lightning flashed overhead. The strike killed Johnson and hit the third man in the eye. Withers was lucky. He suffered only a scorched hat.

To prevent stampedes, some cowboys soothed the longhorns with singing. Trail drivers crooned songs their mothers had taught them, hymns, ballads, fiesta songs, and tunes they made up with sad or funny stories.

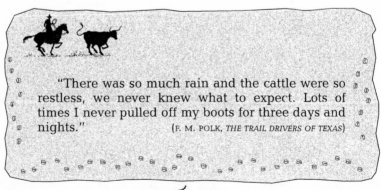

"There was so much rain and the cattle were so restless, we never knew what to expect. Lots of times I never pulled off my boots for three days and nights." (F. M. POLK, *THE TRAIL DRIVERS OF TEXAS*)

They stamped every night that came
And did it without fail.
Oh, you know we had a circus
As we all went up the trail.

The music varied because so did the men. An outfit herding cattle consisted of cowboys who were African American, White, Hispanic, and Native American. Some were law-abiding citizens; others were outlaws on the run. The educated and the uneducated, runaways, cattle owners, hired hands—they ate, slept, and rode together. Each depended upon the other to do his job and to help when someone was in trouble.

Depending upon the weather, cowboys often found it pleasant to sleep under the stars. Drovers caught shuteye before it was their turn to ride night watch. Some cowhands encircled bedrolls with ropes made of horse hair. They believed that rattlesnakes would not cross a cord made of hair.

Skunks were another dreaded pest. From Texas to Kansas, the meat-eating black-and-white fiends caused harm.

"The skunk is carnivorous and his mouth, shaped like that of a raccoon, is furnished with a beautiful set of sharp white teeth," wrote Lieutenant Colonel Richard Dodge. "He is nocturnal in his habits, and very fearless, penetrating in search of food into camps and tents while the inmates are asleep. In such cases he is greatly to be feared, for, so far from keeping away from sleeping men, he will, if he finds nothing more to his taste, deliberately commence devouring the hand, face, or any uncovered part of the sleeper."

While stationed at Fort Dodge, Kansas, during 1872–73, Lieutenant Colonel Dodge knew of sixteen cases of skunks biting men. All proved fatal because the skunks gave the deadly rabies virus to the individuals.

A cowboy lived exposed to skunks, rattlesnakes, lice, spiders, sun, hail, wind, rain, dust, lightning, and tornadoes twenty-four hours a day, seven days a week. Driving cattle took weeks, if not months. When a cowhand reached Abilene or Dodge City, he threw away his worn, torn trail clothes and bought new ones.

River crossings and stampedes broke the daily routine of walking beside cattle for several hours each day. Moving cattle and horses across rivers was either an easy swim or a scary event. High, fast water swept away cowboys and longhorns alike to their deaths.

Trail bosses chose crossings with care. Most drovers riding the Chisholm Trail traversed the Red River into Indian Territory at the Red River Station. The station lay east of a bend in the river. This bend slowed the water's flow, making it easier and safer to cross.

A good lead steer was a cowboy's best friend. The animal would bravely plunge into the water and guide the rest of the herd to the other side.

The Red River, like the South Canadian River, had areas with treacherous quicksand. Animal, man, or chuck wagon became stuck if they moved too slowly. At worst, they would sink into the shifting sands and drown.

Cowboys and their horses would swim alongside the longhorns to keep the animals moving in one

Drovers watering cattle on their way up the Chisholm Trail.

direction. Some drovers thought the best method for crossing deep rivers was to hold on to the tails of their horses. The animals pulled the cowboys through the water like a train pulls its caboose along a track.

A cowboy named Mr. Woods always used this method to traverse deep waters. On one particular trip, though, he ran into trouble. About halfway across a wide river, Woods' horse got his hind leg caught in the saddle stirrup. This caused the animal to swim in a circle. Woods feared that he and his horse would soon drown. He took his knife and cut the leather stirrup loose, but the panicked horse swam free without him.

Woods grabbed the next-closest tail. It belonged to a big, bad, long-horned steer. The cowboy held on tightly as the mighty-horned animal pulled him across the river. When they reached shore, Woods scrambled

for a nearby tree with the angry steer right behind him.

"Trail drivers had many narrow escapes," wrote W. F. Cude, "and were exposed to many storms, cyclones, hail and all kinds of weather, stampedes of cattle, running over ditches and bluffs at night. Some men never came back, but were buried along the lonely trail among the wild roses, wrapped only in their bed blankets."

Despite the hardships, most cattle drovers enjoyed life on the trail. When the time came to run another herd, the men were "rarin' to go."

Chapter 8

Life on the Wild and Woolly

Earlier in the day, Sol West had ordered his trail cook to set up the grub wagon at Hell Roaring Creek, Indian Territory. Hot coffee waited for the men. It was April 6, 1874. All day it had been snowing or raining, and a cold north wind bore down on the outfit like a freight train.

Sol West, the trail boss, chose Hell Roaring Creek because of the abundant grass and water. Each day West selected the bed ground and ordered the cook to ride ahead and set up camp.

In most outfits, ten cowhands, in addition to the trail boss and cook, drove the herd. A wrangler took care of the remuda of spare horses—usually six horses for every cowboy. Two men rode point at the front of the herd. They directed where the herd should go. Swing men rode in the middle, on either side of the herd, and flank men rode toward the rear. These cowboys kept the herd moving at a steady pace and watched for animals that strayed from the main herd. At the tail end of the herd, drag riders choked on the

43

dust caused by the hundreds of animals that walked ahead of them. The youngest and least experienced men rode drag.

Cowboys allowed cattle to graze as they moved along. They wanted the longhorns to gain weight on the trail so that they weighed more at the railroad depot. The more the animals weighed, the more money the trail boss earned.

Around 3:00 in the afternoon, Sol West and the first of his herd were only one hundred yards from camp. The longhorns had walked fifteen miles that day. Suddenly, a blizzard of blinding snow hit. The freezing north wind caused the longhorns to turn southward, away from camp. Cowboys rushed to keep the animals moving northward toward Hell Roaring Creek.

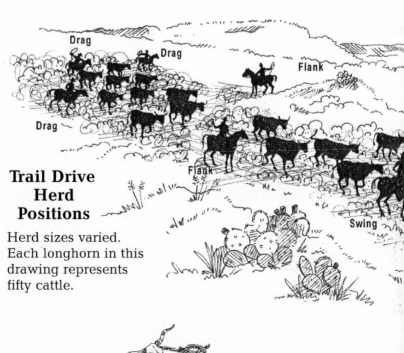

Trail Drive Herd Positions

Herd sizes varied. Each longhorn in this drawing represents fifty cattle.

"I knew we were in for a bad night of it and there was not a man in the outfit over twenty years old," wrote West. "We held the cattle back as best we could until after dark. In the meantime, the horses ridden by the boys had actually frozen to death ... My horse was the last to go down."

West and his men found themselves on foot. They spotted a light in the distance and started walking toward it. Settlers living in a two-room dugout, a home cut into a small hillside, welcomed the outfit and fed them supper.

The next morning West woke to a foot and half of snow and ice on the ground. He found the longhorns in good condition, but the entire remuda of sixty-five horses had perished in the blizzard. Other cowboys in the outfit had survived the blizzard by building a fire

Swing

Chuck Wagon

Wrangler   Remuda

Point

Trail Boss

Point

in a shelter of trees. They had kept it burning all night long.

West traded longhorn steers for more horses so that the crew could complete their trip to Kansas. Due to the blizzard, Sol West made only a $1.50 in profit that trip, but he was lucky to have escaped with his life.

On the plains and prairies, wood was not always available to burn. The men who found wood for their fires during blizzards were lucky. Many times, outfits rode through country rich with grasses and wildflowers but few trees. Timber grew along the creeks and rivers. If the cowboys saw trees in the distance, they hoped to find water.

When there was no wood to burn, the men collected dried buffalo dung. Dried dung was placed in "the cradle," a sheet of canvas stretched underneath the chuck wagon, for the cook to use. The chips burned hot and odorless.

Cowboys who worked during the early cattle drives saw lands teeming with wildlife. Prairie chickens, turkey, deer, antelope, elk, coyotes, wolves, rabbits,

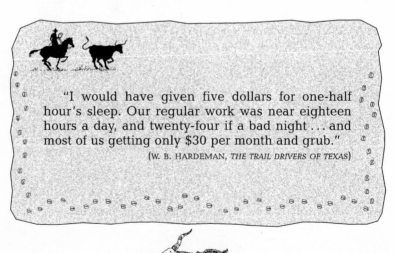

"I would have given five dollars for one-half hour's sleep. Our regular work was near eighteen hours a day, and twenty-four if a bad night . . . and most of us getting only $30 per month and grub."

(W. B. HARDEMAN, *THE TRAIL DRIVERS OF TEXAS*)

and prairie dogs were commonly seen on the trail. Bison, or buffalo, herds were so large that they caused traffic jams. Outfits were forced either to wait for hours as the buffalo herds passed or to attempt to drive the bison away. Antelope, deer, elk, and wolves also mixed with the rolling herds of buffalo. Drovers had to watch that their longhorns and horses did not join the menagerie.

Sometimes a cowboy took a break from his daily routine to hunt the wild game. Fresh deer, rabbit, or turkey broke the monotony of eating pinto beans, called "Pecos strawberries," dried beef, and sourdough biscuits every day for weeks on end. Outfits rarely killed and ate one of their own longhorns, because it meant less profit at the end of the trail. If a cowpoke was lucky, "cookie" might fix canned tomatoes or mix together a dessert called "spotted pups"— rice with raisins.

Oh, it's bacon and beans almost every
  single day
And I'd sooner be a-eatin' prairie hay.
Coma ti yi yippy, yippy yay, yippy yay!
  Coma ti yi yippy, yippy ya!
On a ten-dollar horse and a forty-dollar saddle
I started out a-punchin' those long-horned
  cattle.
Coma ti yi yippy, yippy yay, yippy yay!
  Coma ti yi yippy, yippy ya!
>   —"The Old Chisholm Trail"
>   Traditional Song

Chapter 9

Good-bye, Long-horned Critters

"It was a horrible yet fascinating sight," wrote Amanda Burks. "Frantic cowboys did all in their power to stop the wild flight, but nothing but exhaustion could check the stampede. By working almost constantly the men gathered the cattle in about a week's time. They were all thrown into one big herd, and the roar of hoof-beats of two thousand milling cattle was almost deafening."

In spring 1871, Amanda Burks' husband asked her to ride up the trail with him from Texas to Kansas. Mrs. Burks endured stampedes, hail storms, prairie fires, and swollen rivers. When she and her husband reached Kansas, the price for cattle was so low they decided to wait and see if the prices would improve. By December it was so cold that the young cattle lost their horns. Cowboys had to chop away ice so the longhorns could drink. The Burks sold their bone heads for the going price and headed back for Texas.

Fifteen years later, Mary Taylor Bunton rode the Chisholm Trail with her husband, Howell Bunton.

Unlike Amanda Burks, she did not have to worry about ornery longhorns.

"I traveled most of the time with what was known as the 'lead herd' and camped with it every night," wrote Mary Bunton. "This one herd consisted of some several thousand head of heifer yearlings, all red Durhams of the same size, age and color... It made a beautiful sight on the trail. To me, it looked as if a dark-red velvet carpet with its wide border of green grass was stretched just as far as the eye could see."

Mary Bunton rode the Chisholm Trail in 1886. She endured the hot sun, rain, and rattlesnakes—all the hardships of the trail except stampedes. Heifer yearlings were one-year-old females. These critters were pussycats compared to the jumpy, skittish, stubborn, rough-and-tumble longhorns.

Howell Bunton, like most cattlemen in the 1880s, raised other cattle breeds instead of longhorns.

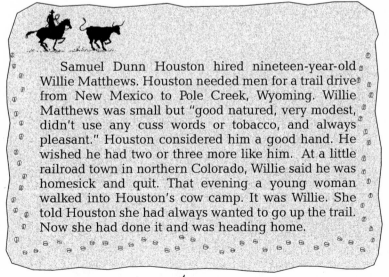

Samuel Dunn Houston hired nineteen-year-old Willie Matthews. Houston needed men for a trail drive from New Mexico to Pole Creek, Wyoming. Willie Matthews was small but "good natured, very modest, didn't use any cuss words or tobacco, and always pleasant." Houston considered him a good hand. He wished he had two or three more like him. At a little railroad town in northern Colorado, Willie said he was homesick and quit. That evening a young woman walked into Houston's cow camp. It was Willie. She told Houston she had always wanted to go up the trail. Now she had done it and was heading home.

49

Durhams, called shorthorns, came from England. In comparison to the slender longhorns, Durhams looked like four fat hot-dogs glued together.

Ranchers no longer wanted the skinny, sway-backed, temperamental longhorn. The bone-headed critter had lost its place on the cattle trail. It was sliding down the slippery slope toward extinction.

Ranchers were "grading up" their longhorn stock with Durhams, Brahmans, Angus, and Herefords. They wanted cattle that produced more beef and matured in a couple of years. Animals that weighed more sold for higher prices, and the owners made more money. Longhorns did not reach their full weight and height for eight years.

Cowboys preferred to handle small-horned cattle. Long, sharp projections made for dangerous work. A bad-tempered steer could gore a horse and its rider. It could also injure other longhorns in the herd.

When longhorns reached Kansas, the animals were loaded into railroad cars. Their lengthy topknots took up a lot of space. As a result, fewer bone heads could be placed in the stock car, because the loaders had to accommodate lengthy horn spreads. With shorthorns, loaders could place more cattle in a railroad car and, therefore, ship more animals to market.

Longhorns also possessed a skittish nature. After walking the wide-open prairies, these high-strung animals rebelled against confinement inside boxes. Steers caused the most problems. The older they got, the meaner they grew. But cattle owners preferred steers. They gained the most weight on the grassy walk northward.

50

"A ride on the railroad made a great strain on their nervous system," wrote Charles Martin, "and an excited steer trying to plunge around in a crowded stock-car was pretty sure to damage some of his companions in misery."

Some ranchers did not want to completely erase the longhorn breed, so they mixed longhorns with other cattle breeds, such as Brahman. Ranchers wanted to retain the longhorns' ability to endure harsh conditions plus its natural resistance to Texas fever.

Over time, the pure longhorn breed began to disappear from the western landscape. By 1890, raising longhorns was no longer practical. Slab-sided and bony, they did not produce the needed beef for a modern world.

Twenty years later, few longhorns existed. Most had been slaughtered or bred out of existence. After four hundred years, their place in history seemed forever lost.

Chapter 10

MODEL TS AND CRATED LONGHORNS

Spots, Old Red, Buttercup, and Old Broad are names of the better-known longhorns that went to the Wichita Mountains Wildlife Refuge. These four were part of the original thirty that arrived in August 1927.

Just seven years earlier, a small group of determined people had decided to rescue the longhorn breed from extinction. By the 1920s, longhorns had almost disappeared from the United States.

Will Barnes was a U.S. Forest Service employee who liked the sway-backed, bony-hipped, long-horned critter. For eight years, from 1919 to 1927, Barnes worked to find funding for the project. Finally, Senator John B. Kendrick listened with a sympathic ear. Kendrick had once been a cowboy who drove cattle from Texas and later built a ranch in Wyoming. With the senator's support, the Sixty-ninth Congress gave $3,000 to purchase longhorn cattle for the Wichita Mountains Wildlife Refuge.

With money to spend, Barnes wasted no time beginning his trek for bone heads. He and a fellow

Forest Service employee, John Hatton, traveled through south Texas during July 1927. They wanted to find enough cows, bulls, and mighty-horned steers to create a small herd.

The two men looked at 5,000 head of cattle. Few were pure longhorns. Near Hebbronville, Texas, they discovered the "best steer in the State of Texas." Unfortunately, a movie company thought the same thing. Filmmakers were producing westerns, and they wanted real longhorns in the background of their mo-

Longhorns arrive at the Wichita National Forest and Game Preserve in Model T trucks.

—Wichita Mountains Wildlife Refuge

53

tion pictures. The film studio had more money to spend than Barnes, and so the "best steer in Texas" became a movie star.

Finally, through hard work and persistence, Barnes and Hatton collected thirty longhorns to ship to the wildlife refuge. First the longhorns had to stop at Fort Worth, Texas, for a dipping to rid them of ticks.

"The two shipments were concentrated at Fort Worth and held for fifteen days," wrote Hatton, "during which time they were dipped three times, at seven-day intervals, to free them from the deadly Texas-fever tick... Repeated handling of the cattle made them vicious and it became some ordeal to put them through the chutes and dips."

Hundreds of people traveled to the stockyards to view the animals. Five movie companies also stopped to shoot film.

By mid-August it was time to ship the animals to the wildlife refuge in Oklahoma. Cowhands loaded the animals onto the railroad cars. They traveled to Cache, Oklahoma, and arrived at the refuge on Thursday, August 18, 1927. Tempers and horns flew in the stock cars. Sadly, one cow was trampled during the journey. She died soon after arriving in Cache.

Model T trucks delivered crates of longhorns to the wildlife refuge. The animals were individually boxed like rare diamonds. Twenty years earlier, similar-looking crates had delivered bison to the refuge. A seed herd of fifteen buffalo had arrived from Bronx, New York, in October 1907. Numbering fewer than six hundred bison in the United States, the bison teetered on the brink of extinction. Within ten years' time, the

herd grew by 700 percent. Perhaps the Wichita Mountains Wildlife Refuge could also save the long-horn.

Spots, one of the original thirty that arrived in August 1927, gained a reputation as the meanest bull in the group. His temperament proved unpredictable. He charged both people and horses, aiming his top-knot for the stomach area. Old Red, a cow, lived the longest. She died on January 9, 1940. Buttercup was the next-oldest living survivor of the original herd. She birthed eight calves during the twelve years she lived at the refuge.

Old Broad was a steer that developed droopy

"Old Broad" had his horns damaged by being thrown to the ground too many times.
—Denver Public Library

Herd of longhorn cattle.
—Museum of the Great Plains

horns. When he arrived, he sported the widest spread in the group. His horns measured four feet, the length of a bathtub.

Some of the animals that arrived in 1927 had a parasite infection known as screwworm. Larvae of the screwworm fly bore into the skin of the animals. If left unattended, the results proved fatal. The cowhands had to rope Old Broad to treat him with medicine.

The big steer enjoyed the treatment about as much as people enjoy a shot at the doctor's office. He fought attempts to handle him. During one session, he dislocated his hip. After being repeatedly thrown to the ground, Old Broad's horns became damaged. Both of his lengthy weapons drooped next to his face like pigtails.

Over the next twenty-five years, the refuge added

more bone heads. Some came from Mexico and others from private Texas ranchers who had kept a few longhorns.

In May 1936, six young longhorns were shipped to the Fort Niobrara National Wildlife Refuge in Valentine, Nebraska. Government officials wanted a second herd in case disease or disaster hit the Oklahoma preserve. One bull, four cows, and one steer traveled from the Wichita Mountains Wildlife Refuge to start a new herd. Over time, more Oklahoma longhorns traveled to Valentine, Nebraska.

Both the Wichita Mountains Wildlife Refuge and the Fort Niobrara National Wildlife Refuge worked hard to preserve the longhorn. Admiration for the animal grew. Bone heads appeared on more and more private ranches. Cattlemen raised them for the enjoyment of owning the historic breed. Others sold them for beef.

Recently, though, controversy has surrounded the animals. The United States Fish and Wildlife reviewed its plans for the Niobrara Refuge and decided that the longhorns were damaging the grasslands.

On November 11, 2000, steers, cows, and calves from moved Fort Niobrara to Fort Robinson State Park. An old-fashioned cattle drive herded the animals 180 miles from Valentine to Crawford, Nebraska. Citizens lined Valentine's main street as cowhands drove the longhorns through town.

Some have questioned whether the Texas longhorns should remain at the Wichita Mountains Wildlife Refuge. Unlike the bison and elk, the longhorn is not considered a native species. Others feel

the longhorn is unique to the North American continent. Its ancestors traveled from Spain over five hundred years ago. As it spread through Mexico and Texas, it developed into a distinctive breed.

Bony from hip to horn, the longhorn carved a noble place in history. It has touched the lives of men and women like few animals ever have. Cowboys and cowgirls survived stampedes, dangerous river crossings, lightning, and blizzards to make their living selling longhorns.

*I woke up one morning on the Old
Chisholm Trail,
Rope in my hand and cow by
the tail.
Coma ti yi yippy, yippy yay,
yippy yay!
Coma ti yi yippy, yippy ya!*

Glossary

Angus—a breed of cattle that is black in color and has no horns. Originally from Scotland.

beeves—full-grown steers, bulls, or cows that will be used for meat.

bison—a large animal with a hump and short horns. Commonly called a *buffalo*.

brackish—salty-tasting.

bulls—male cattle.

carnivorous—a word used to describe an animal that eats flesh.

Chisholm Trail—a major route for herding cattle from Texas to Kansas. Named after Jesse Chisholm.

chuck wagon—a wooden wagon pulled by horses that held food, water, medicine, tools, and other supplies. The camp cook was in charge of the chuck wagon.

cloven hoof—an animal hoof that is divided into two main parts.

cows—female cattle.

doggies—a cowboy's word for cattle.

drover—a person who drives cattle.

59

dugout—a shelter or home made by digging a large hole into the side of a hill.

Durham—a breed of cattle that is generally red or white in color and has short horns. Originally from England.

extinct—no longer alive.

freighter—someone who travels to different places with items, such as flour, coffee, and cloth, to sell.

greenhorn—an inexperienced cowhand.

immunity—able to resist disease or illness.

Indian Territory—an area reserved by the United States government for Native American tribes to reside. Throughout history the boundaries changed. In 1907 it became part of the state of Oklahoma.

instinct—a trait that an animal is born with.

Jayhawkers—Kansas anti-slavery guerrilla fighters who fought during the Civil War.

keratin—a protein that forms fingernails and toenails in humans and horns and hooves in animals.

knoll—small hill.

lasso—a stiff rope used by cowhands to capture cattle.

mandible—the organ of an insect that is used for biting.

mesquite—a shrub that grows in tight clumps known as *thickets*. This plant is found in Mexico and the southwestern part of the United States.

mossy horn—normally refers to an older steer. As they age, the bases of their horns look cracked and gnarled.

nocturnal—active during the nighttime.

prairie—the grassy, treeless area of the central part of the United States.

prairie dog—a small animal that burrows in the ground. It has a short, shrill bark like a dog.

prairie schooner—a covered wagon.

predator—an animal that hunts and eats other animals.

quarantine—to keep people or animals away from others to prevent a disease from spreading.

quicksand—a mass of loose, shifting sand mixed with water. People and animals sink into the sand until they are covered over by it.

rabies—an infectious virus that attacks the central nervous system. Rabies is often carried by mammals, especially skunks, raccoons, foxes, and bats.

Red River Station—a trading post on the Red River. It was located at the area where the cattle and cowboys crossed from Texas into Indian Territory.

running iron—a long, slender branding iron that was often used by cattle thieves to change brands.

rustler—cattle thief.

screwworm—the larvae of a blow fly that burrows into the skin of animals and humans.

Shawnee Trail—an early cattle trail that ran through the eastern part of Indian Territory into Texas.

shorthorn—a name for cattle with small horns. Also a nickname for cowboys who did not know how to handle longhorn cattle.

slicker—a type of long, loose raincoat worn by cowhands.

steer—a male that has been castrated. When the animal is young, its testicles are removed.

stockyard—an enclosed area to hold livestock.

WANT TO READ MORE?

Freedman, Russell. *Cowboys of the Wild West*. Clarion, 1985.

> An excellent book on how cowboys lived, ate, and worked.

Gibbons, Gail. *Yippee-Yay! A Book About Cowboys and Cowgirls*. Little Brown, 1998.

> A factual book about cowhands and how they drove cattle to markets.

Gunderson, Mary. *Cowboy Cooking*. Capstone Press, 2000.

> Make the recipes that chuck wagon cooks used to feed hungry cowboys.

Knowlton, Laurie Lazzaro. *Why Cowboys Need a Brand*. Illustrated by James Rice. Pelican Publishing, 1996.

> Slim Jim owns a ranch but cannot think of the perfect brand.

Pinkney, Andrea Davis. *Bill Pickett, a Rodeo Ridin' Cowboy*. Illustrated by Brian Pinkney. Harcourt Brace, 1996.

> This picture book tells the biography of Bill Pickett, an African-American cowboy and rodeo star. Pickett invented a unique method of subduing cattle.

Sandler, Martin W. *Vaqueros: America's First Cowmen.* Henry Holt, 2001.

> Vaqueros of Mexico and the southwestern United States were the first to work with Spanish cattle.

Sanford, William R. *The Chisholm Trail in American History.* Enslow Publishers, 2000.

> Gives a general overview of life on the famous trail.

Savage, Candace. *Born to be a Cowgirl: A Spirited Ride Through the Old West.* Tricycle Press, 2001.

> Tells little known tales of women who rode the trail and worked the ranches.

Schanzer, Rosalyn. *The Old Chisholm Trail: A Cowboy Song.* National Geographic Society, 2001.

> No one knows who wrote the original "Old Chisholm Trail" song. Over the years, cowboys have added their own verses. Schanzer has illustrated a picture book version of the tune.

Schlissel, Lillian. *Black Frontiers: A History of African American Heroes in the Old West.* Simon and Schuster, 1995.

> Historical photographs complement the stories about African-American cowboys and other frontier men and women.

Webber, Desiree Morrison. *The Buffalo Train Ride.* Illustrations by Sandy Shropshire. Eakin Press, 1999.

> Tells how the Wichita Mountains Wildlife Refuge saved the bison from extinction.

Bibliography

Books:

Anonymous. *A Visit to Texas: Being the Journal of a Traveller Through Those Parts Most Interesting to American Settlers with Descriptions of Scenery, Habits, & c.* Ann Arbor, Michigan: University Microfilms, Inc., 1834, 1966.

Bates, Ed F. *History and Reminiscences of Denton County.* Denton, Texas: McNitzky Printing Co., 1918, 1976.

Benton, Jesse James. *Cow by the Tail.* Boston: Houghton Mifflin Company, 1943.

Bunton, Mary Taylor. *A Bride on the Old Chisholm Trail in 1886.* San Antonio, Texas: The Naylor Co., 1939.

Cowboy Songs and Other Frontier Ballads. Collected by John A. Lomax. New York: Sturgis & Walton, 1910, 1917.

Dale, Edward Everett, and Morris L. Wardell. *History of Oklahoma.* New York: Prentice-Hall, 1948.

Debo, Angie, ed. *The Cowman's Southwest: Being the Reminiscences of Oliver Nelson, Freighter, Camp Cook, Cowboy, Frontiersman in Kansas, Indian Territory, Texas, and Oklahoma, 1878-1893.* Glendale, California: The Arthur H. Clark Co., 1953.

Dobie, J. Frank. *The Longhorns.* Illustrated by Tom Lea. Austin, Texas: University of Texas Press, 1997. (Original publication date is 1941.)

Dodge, Richard Irving. *The Plains of the Great West and Their Inhabitants: Being a Description of the Plains, Game, Indians &c. of the Great North American Desert.*

65

New York: Archer House, 1959. (Original publication date is 1877.)

Emrich, Duncan. *The Cowboy's Own Brand Book*. Illustrated by Ava Morgan. New York: Thomas Y. Crowell, 1954.

Evans, Edna Hoffman. *Written with Fire: The Story of Cattle Brands*. New York: Holt, Rinehart and Winston, 1962.

Fletcher, Baylis John. *Up the Trail in '79*. Norman, Oklahoma: University of Oklahoma Press, 1968.

Gard, Wayne. *The Chisholm Trail*. Illustrated by Nick Eggenhoffer. Norman, Oklahoma: University of Oklahoma Press, 1954.

Haley, J. Evetts. *Charles Goodnight: Cowman and Plainsman*. Illustrated by Harold Bugbee. Norman, Oklahoma: University of Oklahoma Press, 1949.

Hoig, Stan. *Jesse Chisholm: Ambassador of the Plains*. Niwot, Colorado: University Press of Colorado, 1991.

McCoy, Joseph G. *Historic Sketches of the Cattle Trade of the West and Southwest* (1874). Edited by Ralph P. Bieber. Glendale, California: Arthur H. Clark, 1940.

Nevins, Allan. *The Emergence of Modern America, 1865-1878*, vol. 8, *A History of American Life*. New York: Macmillan Company, 1927.

Prose and Poetry of the Livestock Industry with Outlines of the Origin and Ancient History of Our Live Stock Animals. Prepared by the National Live Stock Association. New York: Antiquarian Press, 1959. (Original publication date 1904.)

Pukite, John. *A Field Guide to Cows: How to Identify and Appreciate America's Fifty-two Breeds*. New York: Penguin Putnam, 1996.

Quakertown, Denton, Texas, 1870-1922. Denton County Historical Commission, 1991.

Raine, William MacLeon, and Will C. Barnes. *Cattle, Cowboys, and Rangers*. (Originally published under the title *Cattle*.) New York: Grosset & Dunlap, 1930.

Rouse, John E. *World Cattle III: Cattle of North America*. Norman, Oklahoma: University of Oklahoma Press, 1973.

Siringo, Charles A. *A Texas Cowboy; or, Fifteen Years on the Hurricane Deck of a Spanish Pony*. Chicago: M. Umbdenstock & Co., 1885.

Smithwick, Noah. *The Evolution of a State or Recollections of Old Texas Days*. Compiled by his daughter Nanna Smithwick Donaldson. Austin, Texas: Gammel Book Company, 1900. (Microfilm.)

Songs of the Cowboys. Collected by N. Howard Thorp. Boston and New York: Houghton Mifflin, 1908, 1921.

Stephen, Les, and Ward Sullivan. *Cattle Breeds Index*. Hays, Kansas: Research Communications, Inc., 1976.

Thoburn, Joseph B. *A Standard History of Oklahoma, vol. 1*. Chicago: The American Historical Society, 1916.

The Trail Drivers of Texas. Compiled and Edited by J. Marvin Hunter. Nashville, Tennessee: Cokesbury Press, 1925.

Wellman, Paul I. *The Trampling Herd*. Illustrations by F. Miller. New York: Carick & Evans, Inc., 1939.

Articles:

Barnes, Will C., "The Texas Longhorn Preserved from Extinction." *The Journal of Heredity*, vol. 18, no. 10, 1927, pp. 443-446.

———. "Uncle Sam Saves the Longhorn from Extinction." *American Forests*, vol. 33, 1927, p. 171.

Bartnicki, Gene. "The WR Bloodline from Then 'til Now." *Texas Longhorn Journal*, August 1991, p. 8 (4).

Dobie, J. Frank. "The First Cattle in Texas and the Southwest Progenitors of the Longhorns." *Southwestern Historical Quarterly*, vol. 42, no. 2, January 1939. (pages?)

Dooner, John. "The Antique Cattle." *Farm Magazine*, Spring 1964.

Halloran, Arthur. "Additional Longhorn Cattle Management Records from Wichita Mountains Wildlife Refuge." *Proc. Okla. Acad. Sci.*, vol. 42, 1962, pp. 268-271.

———. "The Heritage of the Longhorn." *The Oklahoma Cowman*, September 1967, p. 18 (2).

———. "In the Beginning There Were Longhorns, and There Still Are." *The Oklahoma Cowman*, vol. 6, no. 10, November 1966, p. 8 (2).

Hatton, John. "The Search for the Longhorns." *The*

Producer: The National Live Stock Monthly, November 1927, p. 4 (3).

Hoyt, Alan M. "First Bulls for WR Were Hard to Find." *Texas Longhorn Journal*, March/April 1984, p. 68 (4).

Mendenhall, Don. "The Legendary Longhorn." *Your Public Lands*, Summer 1984, vol. 34, p. 17 (3).

Reed, Estey I. "The Longhorns Roam Again." Source unknown. Arthur Halloran papers. Museum of the Great Plains, Lawton, Oklahoma.

Sanders, Alvin Howard. "The Taurine World: Cattle and Their Place in the Human Scheme—Wild Types and Modern Breeds in Many Lands." *The National Geographic Magazine*, vol. 47, no. 6, December 1925, pp. 591-710.

"Saving the Texas Longhorns." *Literary Digest*, April 16, 1927.

Shelton, Emily Jones. "Lizzie E. Johnson: A Cattle Queen of Texas." *Southwestern Historical Quarterly*, vol. 50, January 1947, pp. 351-366.

Newspapers:

"Longhorns Are on Way to Park: 25 Head of Old-Time Breed Shipped Monday from Fort Worth." *Lawton Constitutional*, Tuesday, August 16, 1927.

Owen, Penny. "Texas Cattle Route Drives Controversy: 'Chisholm' Name Debated by Texans." *The Daily Oklahoman*, December 10, 2001.

"Texas Longhorn Steers Secured for Wichita Mountain Preserve." *Lawton Constitutional*, Friday, August 12, 1927.

Interviews:

Daniels, Claudine. Environmental Education Specialist, Wichita Mountains Wildlife Refuge.

Goodspeed, Decie. Wetumka, Oklahoma. Daughter-in-law to James Madison Dobbs, a cowboy who rode the trails.

Kimball, Joe. Range Biologist, Wichita Mountains Wildlife Refuge.

Klemme, Robert. Chisholm Trail historian.

Olds, Fred. Retired director of the Guthrie Historical Museum (check name).

Pamphlets:

Conservation Note 18. "The Texas Longhorn." United States Department of the Interior. [n.d.]

"The Texas Longhorn: A Living Link with Western History." Produced by the Texas Longhorn Breeders Association of America. [n.d.] Arthur Halloran papers. Museum of the Great Plains, Lawton, Oklahoma.

"Texas Longhorn Centennial Trail Drive, 1866-1966." Texas Longhorn Breeders Association of America, 1966.

Other Records:

"History of Founding Texas Longhorn Herd at Fort Niobrara National Wildlife Refuge, Nebraska." Wichita Mountains Wildlife Refuge papers, National Archives—Southwest Region, n.d.

Letter from Ernest Greenwalt, Acting in Charge, to Regional Director, Bureau of Biological Survey, January 9, 1940. (Regarding death of "Old Red," last of the original longhorns.) National Archives—Southwest Region.

Letter from Harry French, Forest Supervisor, to Fish and Game, Wichita, December 14, 1929. (Regarding Five-Year Report.) National Archives—Southwest Region.

Letter from Harry French, Forest Supervisor, to G., Supervisor, Wichita, May 5, 1931. National Archives. (Concerning Old Broad.) National Archives—Southwest Region.

Letter from Harry French, Forest Supervisor, to Mrs. Sallie Morris Simpson, October 4, 1932. (Regarding Old Broad.) National Archives—Southwest Region.

Letter from Harry French to Chief of Bureau of Biological Survey, U.S. Dept. of Agriculture, Washington, D.C., July 17, 1936. (French went to Chihuahua, Mexico, to purchase three longhorn bulls.) National Archives—Southwest Region.

Letter from George Muchback, Superintendent, Wichita Mountains Wildife Refuge, to Dr. L.S. Smith, Bureau of

Animal Industry, January 25, 1939. National Archives—Southwest Region.

Letter from William Jones, Curator of History, Great Plains Historical Association, to Arthur Halloran, March 13, 1967. Arthur Halloran papers. Museum of the Great Plains, Lawton, Oklahoma. (1,000-pound steer would furnish 540 pounds of meat.)

Longhorn Cattle, 1927. (From Record Book, 1927: Record of how $3,000 of congressional appropriation was expended on longhorn cattle in Devers and Edinburg, Texas.) National Archives—Southwest Region.

Memorandum from John Hatton, Assistant District Forester, to Forest Supervisor, Wichita. Subject: Longhorns, November 6, 1928. National Archives—Southwest Region.

Memorandum from Harry French, Forest Supervisor, to District Forester. Subject: Longhorns, December 3, 1928. National Archives—Southwest Region.

Memorandum from John Hatton, Assistant District Forester, to Forest Supervisor, Wichita. Subject: Longhorns, December 12, 1928. National Archives—Southwest Region.

PR Information sheet, n.d. "1927—$5,000 appropriated for purchase of Texas Longhorn cattle." National Archives—Southwest Region.

PR Information sheet, December 18, 1939, United States Dept. of the Interior, Bureau of Biological Survey. "Texas Longhorns on Federal Areas Recall Frontier Days."

Reports:

Annual Fish and Game Report, 1928. National Archives—Southwest Region.

Fish and Game, Wichita, 1929. National Archives—Southwest Region.

Videos:

The McCasland Foundation. *The Chisholm Trail*. Norman, Oklahoma: Television and Satellite Services at the College of Continuing Education, n.d. Videocassette.

INDEX

Desiree Webber (left) and Sandy Shropshire

This is Webber and Shropshire's second collaboration for Eakin Press. Webber makes her home in Bethany, Oklahoma, and Shropshire lives in Oklahoma City. Both work as librarians when not busy writing, drawing, and speaking.

Chad Payne makes his home on the Chisholm Trail in

Duncan, Oklahoma. His work can be found in numerous galleries throughout the Southwest. Payne is a retired Army officer and a decorated helicopter pilot, who flew during the Vietnam War. "Maverick," the cover illustration, is an example of the "Old West" as it was. Payne enjoys researching and painting the wild, untamed frontier of the past.

74